2017

BIG PICTURE 📷 SPORTS

Meet the
NEW YORK
JETS

BY
ZACK BURGESS

NorwoodHouse🏠Press

CHICAGO, ILLINOIS

NORWOOD HOUSE 🏠 PRESS

P.O. Box 316598 • Chicago, Illinois 60631
For more information about Norwood House Press please visit our website at
www.norwoodhousepress.com or call 866-565-2900.

Photo Credits:
All photos courtesy of Associated Press, except for the following: Topps, Inc. (6, 10 both, 11 top & middle),
Black Book Archives (7, 18, 23), Fleer Corp. (11 bottom), NFL/Jets (22).

Cover Photo: Bill Kostroun/Associated Press

The football memorabilia photographed for this book is part of the authors' collection. The collectibles used
for artistic background purposes in this series were manufactured by many different card companies—
including Bowman, Donruss, Fleer, Leaf, O-Pee-Chee, Pacific, Panini America, Philadelphia Chewing Gum,
Pinnacle, Pro Line, Pro Set, Score, Topps, and Upper Deck—as well as several food brands, including
Crane's, Hostess, Kellogg's, McDonald's and Post.

Designer: Ron Jaffe
Series Editors: Mike Kennedy and Mark Stewart
Project Management: Black Book Partners, LLC.
Editorial Production: Lisa Walsh

LIBRARY OF CONGRESS CATALOGING-IN-PUBLICATION DATA
Names: Burgess, Zack.
Title: Meet the New York Jets / by Zack Burgess.
Description: Chicago, Illinois : Norwood House Press, [2016] | Series: Big
    picture sports | Includes bibliographical references and index. |
    Audience: Grade: K to Grade 3.
Identifiers: LCCN 2015026322| ISBN 9781599537382 (Library Edition : alk.
    paper) | ISBN 9781603578417 (eBook)
Subjects: LCSH: New York Jets (Football team)--Miscellanea--Juvenile
    literature.
Classification: LCC GV956.N37 B87 2016 | DDC 796.332/64097471--dc23
LC record available at http://lccn.loc.gov/2015026322

288N—072016
Manufactured in the United States of America in North Mankato, Minnesota

CONTENTS

Words in **bold type** are defined on page 24.

The Jets celebrate a big play.

CALL ME A JET

A jet airplane takes off with power and speed. It needs great control to land. When the New York Jets play this way, they usually win. That is why Jets fans are so loud and so loyal. They know the players want to win as badly as they do.

The Jets played their first season in 1960. They were part of the **American Football League**. The team was called the Titans. In 1968, quarterback **Joe Namath** led the Jets to their first championship. The team has had many great running backs. Freeman McNeil was one of the best.

JOE NAMATH

QUARTERBACK
JETS

Freeman McNeil looks for an opening in the defense.

There are lots of great seats in the Jets' stadium.

Best Seat in the House

The Jets play at the Meadowlands Sports Complex, in New Jersey. They moved there from New York in 1984. The Jets share their stadium with the Giants. They are the other National Football League (NFL) in the area.

Shoe Box

The trading cards on these pages show some of the best Jets ever.

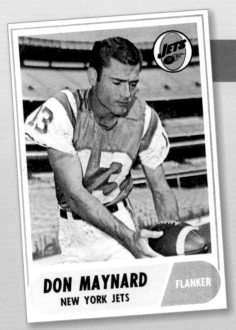

DON MAYNARD

WIDE RECEIVER · 1960–1972
Don was a track star in college. He averaged nearly 20 yards a catch for the Jets.

JOE NAMATH

QUARTERBACK · 1965–1976
Joe was one of the finest quarterbacks ever. He was a great leader with a powerful arm.

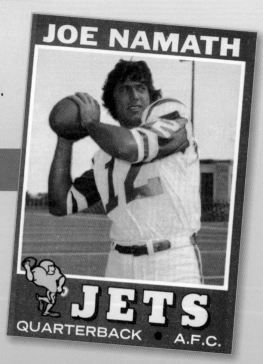

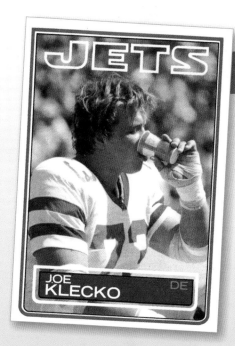

JOE KLECKO

DEFENSIVE LINEMAN · 1977–1987
Joe believed hard work was the key to success. He was named **All-Pro** twice.

FREEMAN MCNEIL

RUNNING BACK · 1981–1992
Freeman was a smooth and powerful runner. He rushed for more than 1,000 yards twice with the Jets.

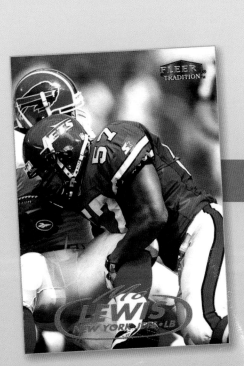

MO LEWIS

LINEBACKER · 1991–2003
Mo was a popular team leader. He was picked for the **Pro Bowl** three times.

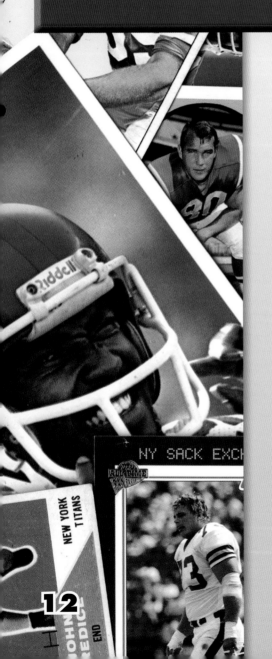

THE BIG PICTURE

Look at the two photos on page 13. Both appear to be the same. But they are not. There are three differences. Can you spot them?

Answers on page 23.

13

TRUE OR FALSE?

Curtis Martin was a star running back. Two of these facts about him are **TRUE**. One is **FALSE**. Do you know which is which?

1. Curtis ran for more than 1,000 yards in each of his first seven seasons with the Jets.

2. Curtis was voted "My Favorite Martin" by Jets fans.

3. Curtis was the oldest player to lead the NFL in rushing yards.

Answer on page 23.

Curtis Martin set many team records.

Jets fans are famous for their team spirit.

GO JETS, GO!

Jets fan wear the team's colors with great pride. Most only do so on Sunday. Some wear green and white all week! All Jets fans go a little crazy on game day. They love to yell one of the NFL's best-known cheers: **J-E-T-S ... Jets! Jets! Jets!**

ON THE MAP

Here is a look at where five Jets were born, along with a fun fact about each.

 1 WESLEY WALKER · SAN BERNARDINO, CALIFORNIA
Wesley averaged 19 yards a catch over 13 seasons.

 2 MARK GASTINEAU · ARDMORE, OKLAHOMA
In 1983 and 1984, Mark had a total of 41
quarterback sacks.

 3 LARRY GRANTHAM · CRYSTAL SPRINGS, MISSISSIPPI
Larry was the captain of the Jets' defense in the 1960s.

 4 EMERSON BOOZER · AUGUSTA, GEORGIA
Emerson was a powerful runner and a great blocker.

 5 BOBBY HOWFIELD · WATFORD, ENGLAND
Bobby once kicked six field goals in a game.

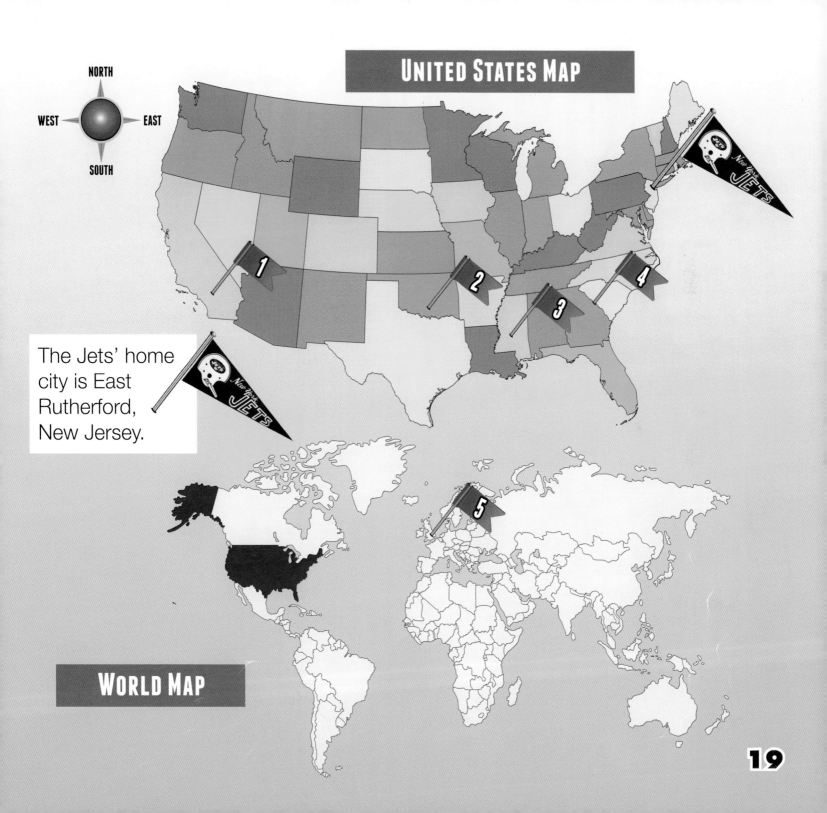

UNITED STATES MAP

The Jets' home city is East Rutherford, New Jersey.

WORLD MAP

Brandon Marshall wears the Jets' home uniform.

Football teams wear different uniforms for home and away games. As the Titans, the team wore blue and gold. After becoming the Jets, the team switched to green and white.

Eric Decker wears the Jets' away uniform.

The Jets' helmet is white and green. It shows a football with *NY* and *JETS* inside of it. The team introduced this design in the 1960s.

The Jets won the Super Bowl after the 1968 season. No one believed Joe Namath when he said his team would beat the mighty Baltimore Colts. But they did, 16–7. Coach **Weeb Ewbank** made a smart game plan for the Jets. They followed it perfectly.

RECORD BOOK

These Jets set team records.

TOUCHDOWN PASSES	RECORD
Season: Ryan Fitzpatrick (2015)	31
Career: Joe Namath	170

RUSHING TOUCHDOWNS	RECORD
Season: **Thomas Jones** (2009)	14
Career: Curtis Martin	58

PASS RECEPTIONS	RECORD
Season: Brandon Marshall (2015)	109
Career: Don Maynard	627

ANSWERS FOR THE BIG PICTURE
The man in the orange jacket on the far left disappeared, #1 changed to #2, and #68's helmet logo changed.

ANSWER FOR TRUE AND FALSE
#2 is false. Curtis was never voted "My Favorite Martin."

FOOTBALL WORDS

INDEX

All-Pro
An honor given to the best NFL player at each position.

American Football League
A rival league of the NFL that played from 1960 to 1969.

Pro Bowl
The NFL's annual all-star game.

Quarterback Sacks
Tackles of the quarterback that lose yardage.

Photos are on **BOLD** numbered pages.

ABOUT THE AUTHOR

Zack Burgess has been writing about sports for more than 20 years. He has lived all over the country and interviewed lots of All-Pro football players, including Brett Favre, Eddie George, Jerome Bettis, Shannon Sharpe, and Rich Gannon. Zack was the first African American beat writer to cover Major League Baseball when he worked for the *Kansas City Star*.

ABOUT THE JETS

Learn more at these websites:
www.newyorkjets.com • www.profootballhof.com
www.teamspiritextras.com/Overtime/html/jets.html